YOU BET NOT CRY!

YOU BET NOT CRY!

"Childhood Abuse – A True Story"

RUFUS LEE BROWN

MRS. QUEENIE MAE BROOKS-JONES-BROWN-MONROE-MYERS

ISBN: 978-1-957009-69-8 (sc)
ISBN: 978-1-957009-70-4 (e)

Library of Congress Control Number: 2022915146

PROLOGUE

"You Bet Not Cry!" is a riveting account of heart-pounding events of childhood abuse in the life of a little girl. It is a revealing truth and tell-all true story. The abuse she endured could no longer be silence. It has taken many years but finally the truth is reveal. "You Bet Not Cry!" is a truth of a seven-year-old girl's abuses by her adoptive parents. This abuses occurred during a time when the Second World War was on the verge starting. It is a mother's story to her son just recently revealed. "You Bet Not Cry!" tells of what a little girl name Queenie Mae Brooks had to endure as a child leading up and into her teenage years. When strangers adopt someone, of course, the family giving their child or children up for adoption expects the best not the worse. It is a difficult situation for anybody or anyone not to know anything about their adopted folks, especially their motives and/or their intentions. Take heart in this true story and help to reveal and prevent abuses. Abuse in any form is damaging and can cause lifelong effects.

I wanted to write a biography of my mother's childhood, when she was a child and into her teenage years. Well, finally this day has arrived. This non-fiction and biography of my mother as a little girl raised by total strangers has become a reality. She experienced more agony than defeat during the total of nine years living in their "house of pain." From her arrival at seven years old until she was married off at the age of sixteen years old, Little Queenie suffered years of abuses. After reading this book, I feel confident that you will help to prevent abuses.

I do not know where I got the idea or came to the impression that my mother had a happy childhood. Maybe, it was because she always told us, her kids, about the joys and adventures of her and her horse, Bandit. Maybe, she only wanted us to remember her as a "little girl and her horse, which was her favorite pet and her best friend. Maybe, just perhaps, she wanted her kids to picture in our mind's eye, a joyous time of her and Bandit doing many exciting things together.

I have always visualized my mother doing fun things and just recently begin to write my own episode in the life of my mother, Queenie Mae Brooks-Jones-Brown-Monroe Myers. My books portrayed a beautiful, little African-American girl, age seven thru 16, having fun with her favorite pet horse, Bandit. As I visualized her words to us, her kids, I concluded in my own mind, no doubt, my mom was happy growing up. Not only my brothers but also my sisters and I were pleased to hear these things as well.

Today, I am writing that it was quite the opposite. Yes, that is correct; my mother's life story was far from a happy childhood. "You Bet Not Cry!" reveals a horrifying experience on a youth. This is where my story begins. I will not use nor pull any punches, but I will reveal the truth, as my mother revealed to me, just recently, as I begin to fill pages after pages of children books of a girl and her pet horse name Bandit and the many fun things she and Bandit enjoyed doing together. Man, I was on a roll – you hear me – but the rolling came to its halt. Now, my mind's direction has taken a different path, at least for now. My mother asks me, "Son, you should write a book about all the abuses your mother experienced. That, my son, will please me more – having the truth exposed," as we sat and talked on the telephone one day during my noontime lunch break. (Currently, we live in different cities, she lives in Gainesville Florida and me, her son, lives in Orlando Florida, approximately one hundred fifteen miles Southeast of Gainesville.

TABLE OF CONTENT BOOK CHAPTERS

TABLE OF CONTENT POETRY – A QUEEN'S TRIBUTE COLLECTION

DEDICATION AND ACKNOWLEDGEMENT

My Loving Departed Mother:
Mrs. Queenie Mae Brooks-Jones-Brown-Monroe-Myers
My Most Beloved Departed Brother:
Mr. Bobby 'Roe' Monroe (Ten years the younger).

ACKNOWLEDGEMENT AND RECOGNITION

To my ten-year-old grandchild Miss Amelia Alicia Herrera-Braddy
whose picture adorn the front cover of this fascinating novel.

To Those Loved and Those That Loved....

Chapter (1)

Little Queenie Mae Brooks Adoption by Seeds of Satan

Therefore, where should I really begin? Ah, yes, the beginning of it all. The beginning when Little Queenie Mae Brooks grandmother, Julia Whitfield, now in her early sixties gave Little Queenie up for adoption at an early age. Queenie's mother, Fanny M. Brooks died when Little Queenie was a young age, possibly five or six years old. Though Little Queenie was from a large family of brothers and sisters, the situation occurred where Little Queenie, the baby of the bunch could not receive the attention and proper education therefore adoption became the Julia Whitfield's solution to help and aid her granddaughter. Her newly adopted parents were learned individuals, knowing how to read and write thus it would seem the young girl would enjoy a wonderful life anew.

My mother was seven years old, at the time, in the late nineteen thirties when she was given up for adoption, several years prior to World War Two was on the verge of catastrophic proportion. Queenie's new African-American family owned their home and its property, free of debt with no mortgage payment. According to my mother, the farm was home to much different kind of farm animals cows, horses, mules, chickens, pigs, ducks, and hogs. This is where and when the real and truthful life of my mother, Little Queenie Mae Brooks, now Little Queenie Mae Jones, now adopted begins. Mrs. Rose E. Jones, a former schoolteacher, her new mother is married to Mr. J.C. Jones, postal worker, and self-employed farmer her new father. Again, I'm moving too fast, jumping the gun, as the expression goes, jumping ahead of mom's conversation about her life as a little girl. So, I decided to listen as my mother revealed more about her life.

My mother does not have photos of her childhood prior to the late nineteen thirties into the mid-nineteen forties. Such cameras that exist today like the ten second Polaroid did not exist during her early childhood. What you will read is a detailed description of what my mother talked to me about as it really happened. Immediately, our conversation begins again.

"Son, your mother did not have a fun life as you described in your children book writings. Though, the script and pictures reflects some good times, my life was far from happiness," says my mother, as I begin to listen intently to what she was telling me. (As I noted earlier, I was on my lunch break at work when I decided to call her. I knew I did not have too much time to talk or listen to her, but I listen to her until it was time to return to work).

The sound of her voice appears dishearten. It was not the gleeful voice of my mother I enjoyed hearing at the other end of the phone when I call her regularly. No, it was solemn and lack cheerfulness.

"But mom, you told us – your children – that you had fun riding your horse Bandit. We, well, especially me – believed that everything was fine. Maybe you did mention it – about the abuses - and I only wanted to hear the fun things," I said to her, my face long and reflecting signs of disappointment – though she could not see my face. If my mother's childhood was not a happy one, then she must have experienced abuses. My mind is sifting like a hundred gold miners sifting for gold in the many rocky mountain streams of the Old West.

"Son, I did not have a fun life. When my grandmother, Julia Whitfield gave me up for adoption at the age of seven years old, I did not know how these people would treat me. Being a little girl, you feel that everyone likes you. I did not know what to expect," she says, pausing briefly, maybe to catch her breath.

"Mom, I surely thought your childhood was fun, maybe your interest in your pet horse, Bandit led me to believe it was a lot of fun," my reply reflecting interest in her comments about her childhood days.

"You **said** your new father was a big man. How big was your new father?" I would ask her. "Mr. J. C. Jones was a huge man, a behemoth of a man, weighing close to three hundred pounds. Mother Rose would call him, "Butterfly Jones" probably his nickname. Anyway, J. C. Jones was dark-skinned in complexion, or had very dark skin and he had what appears like red eyes," announced my mother, describing her new adoptive father - only the exclamation points are missing from the description of him, as she tells me about the man that adopted her. Surely, he was intimidating to almost anybody standing next to him or near him. Being close to three hundred pounds and standing nearly six feet tall makes him a very large individual, no doubt. Especially, from a child's point of view or perspective. No doubt, my mom being such a tiny individual felt overwhelmed by the statue of such a person.

"What do you mean by your new dad having red eyes, mom," I asked her – interjecting and being very inquisitive.

"His eyes were red, son. You know when you don't get enough sleep, how people eyes look all red or blood shot, that is how his eyes were all the time," affirms mom regarding her new dad.

"Oh yeah! I know what you mean," I said, now understanding what she meant.

"He had these red eyes like a devil, and I was frightened by the sight of him. I ran and hid in the outhouse or toilet. That's what they called them back in those days. However, they found me and loaded my things along with me in their automobile and we began our journey to their farm in Long Pond in Alachua County, Florida. (I just learned recently, many of the water spots in the Alachua County area were called "Ponds but having different first names. So, Long Pond was where my adopted parents lived.) There were only a few land owners, six or seven families, African-Americans farmers living close to the Joneses. Mom remembers as if it occurred only recently. Perhaps such events as the ones she will soon reveal are not that hard to forget. She said she was frightened at the sight of him because of his size and red eyes. Something like this could be scary for any kid, I concluded. Mother continues with her story.

"However, I knew this was going to be my father. Maybe he might be a nice man despite his size and looks. My new mother was not fat or skinny but had a healthy look. She appeared to be nice, and I felt she would love me like my own mother before she died and my own grandmother before the adoption," mom states before pausing for a moment, once again. No doubt reflecting on the thoughts of time passed.

"I understand what you are saying, mom. These are total strangers, and you have no knowledge whatsoever about them. After all, you are only a little girl in a new home and in a new place," as I expressed agreement to her new situation.

My mother is not doing too well these days. A very stressful life history has taken its toll on her. Mother having had several heart attacks with stents placed in her heart on different occasions, suffering from type one diabetes, glaucoma in her both eyes and rheumatoid arthritis is a lot to deal with at eighty-four years of age. Recently, she had surgery on her left eye. She has been blind in her left eye for years. This damage occurred at the age of ten when her mother got very angry and hit her with a belt buckle causing severe injury to it. However, I am getting ahead of myself. I will let mom tell her story. I waited for a moment and then she continues. I know I must hang up soon, so I let her tell more of her incredible account of events in her life.

"The address where my grandmother, Julia Whitfield lived was 1215 Julia Street in Jacksonville Florida. We left the city of my birthplace and of my original family and traveled to what will become my new home in Alachua County. I do not know if that country town or area exist anymore but that is where I would live. I remember as we traveled onto their property, a large double gate that kept out or kept in whatever it was built for. Mom's new father, J. C Jones got out the car and walked toward the gate. As he walked forward, he looked back, a glance over his right shoulder, to see if he could see me sitting in the backseat of his automobile. I had just recently awaken from the long drive that put me to sleep, so I had sleep in my eyes, as I looked over the front seat. After opening the large double gate that was part of wired fencing that seem to stretch for long distance on the right and left sides of the large double gate, he returned to the car and proceeded to drive his car on a long winding road that curved to left, then right, then left again, a ride that seems forever before we arrived at the house.

When I finally saw their house, now my new home, it was a large wood frame white house with faded-out slates of wood on the exterior walls. It needed paint very much. It sat on concrete blocks with a deep darkness beneath it. The yard was very large and had some flowers (what kind of flowers, I was too young to tell at that time), lots of weeds and many trees, large and small, possibly oak trees in the front yard and on both sides of the house. The roof had rusty tin covering as if this house has been here for many years.

The inside of the house, once we finally made our way inside, there was a living room area with a long brown sofa and a large brown chair that matched the sofa. There were two colored light brown end tables with flower-colored lamps on them. My new parents home looked old but very comfortable. As I kept walking, I entered a hallway that has three-bedroom. I glance into the first bedroom on the right side of the long hallway that runs from the front of the house to the rear of the house. Will this bedroom be my future bedroom, I thought to myself? The next two bedrooms were on the left side of the long hallway. Once, again my thoughts revisited, which of these bedrooms will become mine, I smiled to myself with much excitement? (I begin missing my brothers and sisters, as I walked the long hallway of my new parent's home.) The house has a front porch with two wooden chairs covered with green cloths and an old brown rocking chair, which looked comfortable. There was a swing hanging from the ceiling that looked comfortable also. The back porch had cut wood, probably for the stove in the kitchen and crates and boxes too. My mind is excitedly thinking about the bedrooms that looked neatly arranged from a little girl point of view. If the bedrooms had cluttered, I would not have known. Again, there's a flashing thought traveling through my mind, which of these three bedrooms will my new father and mother give to their new daughter?

Continuing to admire this new house where I will be staying, I notice that the dining room or dining hall had a large old dining table with four large chairs. They looked old, possibly antique furniture, I guess. There were curtains on all the windows in the house, some with floral colors, were the curtains hanging in the first bedroom on the right of the hallway and other curtains were plain, light blue and yellows colors as observed, hanging in the two bedrooms on the left of the hallway, doing my walk through of the house. My new father and mother were busy unloading the car of my belongings and purchases they made prior to coming to my grandmother's home. They did not ask for my assistance, possibly allowing me the opportunity to view my surroundings. I would receive smiles from them both, assuring me that they were glad to have me there.

"Of course, the outhouse or toilet, as I mentioned earlier was behind the house about twenty feet or more away. My new parents owned many acres of land, how many acres, I can't remember at the moment. This became my new home for nine years. And son as soon as I got there the abuse begin!"

Her voice dropped, maybe she is reflecting on the next set of events, which she will reveal to me. The smiles I received from them both - were unreal. They were fake smiles from two fake people. Misery and disappointment immediately followed.

"That is incredible, mom!" I concurred to her statement of immediate abuse. "You mean they started to treat you bad as soon as you got to their home?" I would ask mother, expressing shock to this newly exposed information.

"Yes honey, as soon as they finish bringing everything in the house from the car and before I could comfortably fit in, the craziness and heart-aching reality kicked in," mom states clearly, showing no hesitation in her reply to my question.

I have to stop here, therefore, I must conclude for now. It is time to return to work. I told mother that I would call her when I get home, so we can talk longer. She agreed and we said our goodbyes.

CHAPTER (2)

Little Queenie Shattered Dreams Leads to A Shattered Life

I arrived home at four o'clock that afternoon, took care of what I needed to then I called mother to continue our conversation. She answers the phone with her very tender voice, a very pleasant voice that makes it so enjoyable to listen to her. I am anxious to hear more, so I sat at my computer and absorbed this revealing conversation. Mom continued where she left off earlier.

"There were three bedrooms in that house, and I did not get to sleep in any of them until more than a year after I arrived there," reveals my mother, her voice went silent, as if she were pondering those stressful days and the emotional impact upon her. Apparently, this is when the mental abuse begins. How she must have pondered sweet thoughts of having her own bedroom, her own bed, her own dresser to put her clothing? How she must have pondered the thoughts of arising every morning to look out the bedroom window and admire the flowers, birds dashing and bees flying from flower to flower, the butterflies of many assorted colors fluttering about outside her bedroom window like any normal child would do. Imagine the ghastly reality and disappointment for such a little girl. This little girl denied one of three bedrooms, which mom mentioned earlier that looked nice. So, where did Little Queenie sleep if not in one of the three bedrooms? I pondered.

"Mom, you are telling me that it was more than a year before you were given a bedroom?" I asked her immediately.

She continues, "I slept on an old army cot! I slept on an old army cot, son, that was set up in the dining room. That became my bedroom for more than a year and then I finally got the bedroom that was separate from their side of the house or at the front right side of the hallway." My mother's voice getting stern, as if she thought she would never get one of the three bedroom and finally live her life as a little girl should live. I could sense terrible disappointment in her voice. Why not a bedroom of her own? What were these people doing to this little girl? For more than one year sleeping on an old army cot! Wow! That is so cruel as one or two bedrooms are empty with no one using them.

"What other abuses, were you subjected to, mom?" I asked mom another question regarding her devastating childhood. I needed to know the other shocking events in my mother's life.

"I remember my new mom kicking me after I accidentally drop and broke one of her bowls. I was still seven years old. It was an accident, you know, accidents does happens. She kicked me hard, son - looked me straight in my eyes, commanded me, "gal, you bet not cry!" She stood there for a moment to see if I would shed any tears and then she walked way. That was my first time hearing those words, but it would not be the last time. It seems as if every time they abused me, they always told me, "gal, you bet not cry!" mother informed me.

"How could Rose make such a harsh demand to you stating such nonsense, "you bet not cry!"

How can you not cry after she kicked you so hard? What are these people thinking?

You are definitely being abused by your so-called new parents," I added immediately to this horrific scene described.

"Whenever they abused me, those words always flowed from their mouths," continued mother's conversation with me. I can sense the frustrations mom must have experienced during those times. She is just a kid and Rose, and J. C. Jones is treating her very badly. There is more, as mom continues.

"I remember as days went by, they would send me into the cotton fields to pick cotton and into the cucumbers and squash fields to pick cucumbers and squash. All day, it seemed, I toiled in fields of cotton, cucumbers, and squash. I became their little slave girl," mother proceeded to inform me.

"It would seem that your adoptive parents should have adopted a boy instead of a girl. The chores you mention are things one would expect a boy to perform," I said after she concluded her comment.

"As I grew older, they worked me as if I was a man. I plowed the fields, following behind horses far larger than me. Everything one would expect a man to do, I had to do," she said.

I immediately interjected, interrupting mom's conversation, because I am curious as to what else her new parents did to her. I do not want to lose my thought on this important matter.

"Mom, besides the mental abuse what other physical abuses were you subjected to?" I quickly interjected. Immediately, she told me of more devastating abuses. She told me her mother would whip her with several peach tree limbs tied together. That signifies to me, her mother's intent to whip my mother for a long time. By tying these peach tree limbs together with tobacco strings, so the limbs do not break as easy. My mother told me that Rose hit her in the head with her fist, then denied her to cry. All the abuses that mother mention had to be very painful, indeed.

"This is an incredible account of your childhood, mom," I said to her as I pondered on the damaging experiences she endured. "Rose definitely wanted you to feel the pain from those peach tree limbs by tying them together," I continued as the abuses on my mother sink into my mind and into my heart. I truly feel much sympathy for mother's devastating childhood.

She also told me her new dad, Mr. J.C. Jones tied her to the bed and whipped her. He also slapped her in the face and he too, just like Rose, told her, "gal, you bet not cry!"

Also, her father whipped her with a cow whip! Wow, a cow whip! If anyone has seen any old westerns or cowboy movies, then they would know what a cow whip looks like and what it can do. These cow whips are necessary items to keep the cows/cattle heading in the direction of the person using the cow whip. She told me her father would tie her to a tree with her back towards him and whip her. One abuse after another and "you bet not cry!"

Imagine that, please. These are just some of the physical abuses she endured. "You Bet Not Cry!" clearly shows the devastating truths of my mother childhood abuses. To put it bluntly - mom said her life was a "living hell!"

"Up until this time in my life, I still have not started going to school yet," as my mother resumes her story. This no doubt troubled her because Rose was a learned individual, knowing how to read and write, as well as her husband. In addition, Little Queenie's grandmother, Julia Whitfield gave her granddaughter up for adoption so that she could get a proper education as I mention at the beginning of mom's story. So, what is the deal? Will mom get the education that she needs to better her life as she grows older? "That is amazing! Both of your parents apparently had some type of education and neither allowed you to attend school so you can learn to read and write," I said as I pondered on how upsetting this could have been for my mother when only a little girl.

"So, mom, when did you begin school?" I asked, curious as to her age when she began to attend school like regular kids.

"I did not begin going to school until I was nine years old. Therefore, two years have gone by before I saw the inside of a classroom. Up until this time, I had become their little slave girl," my mother's voice exploding with all this information. She was convinced they adopted her as a working hand on their farm. She told me that she received no "I love you, my darling little girl or any hugs of comfort" that loving parents give to their children. I hate to say this, but I am getting perturb about all of this. I did not know my mother had to deal with all these difficulties. She did not deserve this kind of behavior. She was only adopted to work. They should have adopted a boy, right! This African American couple are evil Seeds of Satan are as notorious as Russia's Stalin and Germany's Adolph Hitler.

Mother is very exact as the expression goes, telling me of a slavery style childhood. One would expect slaves to perform the many tasks of hard labor - working in the fields all day, doing work one would expect a man to do. What an incredible account of childhood abuses!

"I had to pick cotton, take care of all animals, and milk the eleven cows we had in the barn. Remember, I am only a little kid, and I am working like a grown man." At that moment, she went silent, maybe again, reflecting on her horrible childhood. I hope she is not crying now. I know this is hard for mother to talk about because there is nothing pleasant being told.

Finally, mom said something that seems to enlighten her spirits. She mentioned the birth of

Bandit, the baby colt she will raise. Mom tells of Bandit's birth when she was nine years old. She and Bandit grew together. He became her pet and best friend. There were no other little kids close by to play with. When did she have the time to play? She only has Bandit to bring any kind of joys into her life.

"So, Bandit is born and that is when joy entered your life, huh, mom?" I asked.

"Yes, son, Bandit was my best friend and he made me happy. Our property was so huge; the closes neighbor lived far away. There were no little kids for me to play with. Besides, I was adopted to work not to play," she repeated, convinced that is what she was there for like a broken record on a turntable, as it spins repeating itself over and, over again. "It was work, more work, and more work before going to school and after I got out of school. Work, work, and work!" mom said expressing disgust of a childhood filled with manly chores and no love or affection as a little girl should receive. There is more as mom continues to tell about her early childhood.

"My new father taught me how to ride horses when a little girl so I can help round up the cows in the fields and pastures. I can remember only one helper, but they got rid of him shortly after I arrived. As soon as I get home from school I went to work on the farm. It was always late into the night when I got home from working for my parents. It's like I said son, I became their private little slave girl. The love was not there, just a lot of scolding and hitting. A lot of yelling commands and making demands," says my mother exposing more and more information of these two disappointing adults. The adoptive parents that adopted her, not to be their little girl but to become their little slave girl to do the many chores.

"That is so sad, mom. These people used you to do their work rather than hire people to do it. I feel so sad that you experienced such a terrible childhood," I advised my mother as I sat and listen to this incredible story. However, I know mother has more to tell me. However, I must interrupt mom for a moment. My mother can really talk y'all. I must break into the conversation so I can ask her a question before I forget. Yes, mother is telling all. "You Bet Not Cry!" as the title signifies add clarity to a world of abuses. She is telling me things I never knew about her childhood or about her adoptive parents.

I proceeded to ask my mother, "You said there was only one helper working for your family. Then all the burden of work fell on you, correct? Did they help you, your new mom and dad?" I was very curious as to the extent of their abuses to my mother.

I pictured in my mind, many acres of land fill with cows, mules and horses roaming in pastures. I am thinking of the other farm animals, the chickens, pigs, and the ducks. I am thinking of how these so-called adults can treat a little girl like this as if she is nothing but an object to scold, maltreat and abuse.

My mother starts up again. "Son, those people worked your mother, you hear me. They had to help me because I could not do it all, but I was expected to do every job around the farm, inside the home and outside of the home," mom continues describing those disturbing days.

I am remembering that my mom's adoptive father was a huge man and probably had a huge appetite. Mrs. Rose E. Jones taught my mother how to cook at an early age, so she had an additional burden placed upon her. She must have felt like a miniature David of the Israelites and her adoptive father a giant like Goliath of the Philistines each time she stood before, beside or near this person. My mother is not five feet tall today so, she had to be very short, maybe over four feet tall when she was approaching her teen years.

"I had to collect the eggs, feed the animals, milk the cows, rounded up the cows in the fields, cooked, cleaned the house, you name it I did it. I was there to work," mother states so emphatically, no hesitation in her vocal chords. The emphasis she places on a miserable childhood gone by but not forgotten or will ever be forgotten. The stress had to be tremendous for her, a younger person before her teen years. Little Queenie's parents that adopted her, having so much material possessions, yet showing no love for their adopted daughter.

Wow! How can they be so cruel? That's a double wow!

I interrupted my mother once again. I must hang up now and prepare for the end of another evening. I will call her again tomorrow or the following day to listen to her childhood story. As I said earlier, my mom can really talk. I am always very respectful when I interject a point or ask a question needing an answer.

CHAPTER (3)

A Vicious Rapist and Pedophile
Truest Motives Are Revealed

When I think of the cruel circumstances my mother endured it is hard for me to picture myself going through all she had gone through. I am a man, and she was only a little girl. She endured much. Now, when I look at my mother legs with the many knots and disfigurations, the roughness of her feet, so damaged from years of walking, standing and laborious tasks it is plain to see and picture in my mind, the physical abuses she underwent. One has to see her damaged legs to capture the full scope of what I am talking about. Not good!

Yes, my mother suffered much and endured many agonizing moments. How much of this can a little girl withstand. Yes, I now have time to reflect on the distressing and tormented childhood of her life. She is right, this information need my attention. This information needs publicizing. Any abuse is pain stalking and hard to forget. It has its emotional impact on the body, (my mom's body is worn down), the mind (my mother will never forget the devastating effects of her childhood), and on the soul. Abuse creates anxiety and discomfort in a major way for young and old. Age does not matter. My mother is eighty-four years old and the physical, psychological, and sexual abuses, yes sexual abuses still haunts her. She asked me to write this book so that if anyone reads this book, it will show how abuse affects one's life no matter what his or her age.

Imagine the many nightmares Little Queenie must have had to endure. Imagine having to look at these tormentors of your life, daily. Little Queenie's new parents are treating her not like their daughter but like a slave girl. Imagine, adopted, then abused continuously. Please, just imagine living a fearful existence, even for a little girl, whose parents are not loving and kind.

"You Bet Not Cry!" show how vicious and heartless some people can be. Tell me, can you keep your mouth shut or not shed a single tear if somebody is whipping you?

Can you hold back your emotions if someone punch you in your head or slap you in the face? If parts of your body are being tortured or abused in any manner, will you not cry? Well, picture my mother as a little child going through all these things. This is the "house of disdain."

So, when did Little Queenie and Bandit have fun? Maybe, after Bandit, her horse became old enough for her to ride was probably the best times in her life. Those wonderful times must have occurred while away from this "house of pain" and the stressfulness in her life due to her parents abuses. When she is riding Bandit in the fields and pastures must have help her to dismiss those many, many agonizing moments. Those must have been the good times for my mother that she expressed to her children.

I must restate that school became a reality at age nine. Even though her mother was a well-learned she received no schooling from her. A local schoolteacher agreed to come to the house to pick Little Queenie up and take her to school.

Little Queenie will finally get the education her grandmother, Julia Whitfield wanted her to have. The adoption mainly was for this purpose, so she can get an education.

Being denied an education until nine years old was also a form of abuse. Most kids start school at age five or six not nine years old. Now, that I know my mom is finally in school, I decided to ask mom about the sexual abuses. She has experienced so much by the time she began to go to school and get a proper education like other kids her age. How will she cope? Will she be able to fit in with all the other kids after undergoing such an incredible early childhood filled with abuses and disdain? Life can deal terrible blows, even for young ones that are not able to defend for themselves. These defenseless youth are at the mercy of the evildoers.

It is the following day at twelve noon. I sat in my automobile with the air conditioner running. I am sitting in my 1979 Cutlass Black and Gold Hurst Oldsmobile Coupe. Quickly I ate my lunch which consisted of a couple of bologna sandwiches, a bag of Cheetos, and a can of grape soda. I am anxious to ask my mother about the sexual abuses.

What did this evil man, this very gross person do to my mother? I wanted to know as soon possible. Immediately after downing my lunch, I called long distance to Gainesville, Florida to resume our conversation. Mom answers and we say our hellos. I always ask if she feels like talking about the events in her past life before the conversation start, you know, out of respect. Maybe, she might not feel up to it today. However, mother was ready to provide more facts about her abusive childhood.

"When I was eleven years old, my adopted father raped me!" my mother speaking into the telephone. I cannot see her facial expression, but it had to be one of hurt and anger.

"What!" I exclaimed, trying to phantom the amount of hostility she must have possessed when this sexual abuse happened. I can sense in her voice hurt, yes, a lot of hurt.

Immediately I interrupt, "He raped you, mother!" I responded in shock. I told her she never told us that she was raped but she assured me she did get raped. Maybe she told but I do not remember it or paid attention doing the conversation. Wow! This world is truly mad!

"That is so terrible, mom" I said, shaking my head side to side, not in disagreement to her comment but the shock of hearing this bad news. I proceeded to profane at the sound of this atrocity. I would not curse on the phone, but inside in my mind, to myself. I am getting more and more perturb each time mom tells me of the many abuses. However, I must continue to listen and complete these writings. I cannot let my feelings of anger overpower and cause me to lose focus of what I am doing. This little girl, Little Queenie experienced many terrible acts of abuses. She is living in hell on earth in Alachua County, Florida. Her new parents have brought about incredible damages upon Little Queenie.

I calm down long enough to ask mom the three most asked questions; when, where, and how. She proceeded to tell me when she was eleven years old; her adoptive dad, Mr. J.C. Jones told her to saddle her horse so she can help him round up the cows in the cow pastures. They proceeded to ride on horseback across the fields and into the woods to the area where the cows grazed. The ride was long and far from their home. The area was isolated and away from any people. However, Mr. J.C. Jones had other plans in mind besides rounding up cows. This devious and abusive person was living a lie to his wife and his daughter.

It was there, in the woods of the cow pastures he told her to get down off her horse. The grass and weeds were high and uncut. Immediately, Butterfly Jones got down off his horse, all three hundred pounds and began attacking, pulling, and tugging at Little Queenie clothes. My mother was helpless against this giant. Her so-called father is a monster of incredible gross proportion. She fought back she said but lost. He overpowered the eleven-year-old girl, violated her causing injury to her private area. This big and massive dark-skinned ugly monstrous adult hurt my mother very badly. After Butterfly Jones finished violating her, taking away her innocence, again he commands her, "gal, you bet not cry!" He commanded her to keep her mouth shut and not to ever mention this to nobody, ever. Such an intimidating figure will frighten anybody, even a young person. Butterfly Jones seek to strike fear in the little girl, Little Queenie.

I am very upset as I listen to my mother. At eleven-years old and so helpless. She must have been very frightened and scared. As I think about her attack, I recalled seeing a similar situation, an attempted rape in the movie of a like story. I recall the man and the girl (in the movie) riding their horses into the woods and the man tried forcing himself on the young girl. She fought him off and he got very angry and forced her off his land. She did not get raped. Thank God!

However, my mother could not fight off a huge man of such massive weight. She was at his mercy at eleven years old and alone in the woods. She screamed and yelled for help, but no one heard her. The Jones family owned all this property and there were no neighbors close by. Little Queenie Mae was alone and scared. She tried fighting him off her but lost the battle. He knew exactly where to take her and commit this devious sin. It was premeditated and disgusting.

This is the country folks, and her new father took advantage of the setting. His wife, Rose E. Jones probably thinking her husband and adopted daughter were rounding up cows, something they are accustomed to on a daily basis. Remember, their home sits on many acres (nine hundred plus acres, in fact) which they own. There are no neighbors around to hear Little Queenie's scream nor to help her escape this assault. Where will she go? Nowhere! This evil "house of pain" is the last stop for Little Queenie.

Will Little Queenie remain silent? Will she keep this assault to herself like this monster and vicious pedophile told her? What will Little Queenie do? Put a zipper on her lips, figuratively?

"Momma daddy hurt me! Momma daddy hurt me!" My mother told her new mom as soon as she returned home. There were tears, many tears as she rushed to her adoptive mother. She did cry despite continual instructions not to cry. She did not heed Mr. J.C. Jones commands to keep her mouth shut. She did not remain silent following his orders. No, she ran to her mother crying and hurting, mentally and physically. He had hurt the little girl's vaginal area and there was blood. Mom told me there was blood on her saddle from this giant's malicious assault on her.

Expecting her mother to grab hold of her for protection, expecting embraces and sympathy, instead Rose E. Jones slapped Little Queenie very hard to the face and told her to stop lying.

"Mother, she slapped you after her husband just raped you! That is so evil and diabolical," I said in reply to this very hurtful news.

"Yes, she slapped me, called me a liar and told me I bet not ever accuse her husband of something like that again," mother said, her voice full of conviction. She has been carrying this burden since childhood. She was told by her mother that the blood on her and the blood on her saddle was due to her menstrual cycle. She commanded my mother to stop accusing her husband of nonsense. She told my mother her husband would never do anything like that. She raised her hand to strike mother again but did not. It was merely a threat to let my mom know what will happen if she vocalize such accusations against the man of her life, Rose beloved, Mr. J.C. Jones.

Mom told me her new mother said she was making up lies. She ordered my mother to shut up and stop lying and crying. My mother is a rape victim, and she is trapped in a situation where only Jehovah God and his Son, Christ Jesus can save her.

As I reflected on this rape, I recall still someone else that experienced sexual abuse. I recalled a very well-known celebrity broadcasting on a televised show that a family member raped her. This person was a teen when it happened as well. Tears of hurt flowed down her face as many in the audience studio, and throughout the country looked on as the celebrity revealed the truths.

Rape has long-lasting harmful effects on the victim. Rape can happen to anyone, female or male, adults, and children. It is very damaging physically, and psychologically. My mother is proof of this. I want to think that this assault occurred only once. However, mom continues as she tells me he tried to rape her again, several days later. Wow! This pervert truly sought his own daughter for sexual gratification. Yes, a pervert indeed!

"Mother and I were out in the fields collecting cucumbers and squash. It was at noontime, we knew this because of the way our shadow reflection on the ground. We needed water to drink, so mom sent me to the house to get some water. I did not know Mr. J. C. Jones was in the house, but he was in there. (Butterfly Jones was probably watching Little Queenie from a window in their home and hoping Little Queenie would come to the house. Nasty person, Butterfly Jones!)

While I was in the kitchen, he came toward me and then he grabbed hold of me and carried me to his bedroom. "He attacked you again while his wife was close by working in the fields?" I asked mother about this man's desperate attempt to assault her, yet again.

Mom continues, "He grumbled to me in a low but convincing tone to shut up. But I resisted him as much as I could. I screamed and then he covered my mouth with his huge hand to silence me. "This new dad of yours was a pedophile of the worst kind . He probably was watching you for years, hoping, wishing and waiting for the opportune time for an attack on you," I told my mother while I listen to more destructive information presented.

"His huge hand was too powerful for me to remove from covering my mouth. I kicked and kick, but his massive body felt none of my blows. Me struggling was both futile and useless. He attacked me with Rose in the field not far from the house," said mom as her voice display signs of anguish. The feeling of disgust must have been too much to bear at eleven years old.

This has to be hard for her to talk about. This adoptive dad could care less where his wife was at the time. His lust for Little Queenie outweighed his sanity for what is right. However, mom must get this account of her rapist out -- all of it. She can no longer carry this heavy weight, this burden in her heart or mind. She wants people to know just how abuses can disrupt and destroy one's life. "You Bet Not Cry!" reveals the damaging effects of various types of abuses.

My mother has recalled this behemoth of a man waiting in hiding, awaiting for the opportunity to pounce and attack his own adopted daughter. Wow! Little Queenie is an eleven-year-old girl who have fallen victim to a vicious monster, a filthy pedophile that claims to be her father. Mr. J. C. Jones. He is a pedophile of the worst kind, molesting his own kid for sexual pleasures. Little Queenie resist but her efforts to break away from him is ineffective. She is at the mercy of this mad, mad man, again. How will she recover mental or psychological from these vicious assaults? Must Little Queenie Mae Brooks-Jones suffer again at the hands of her new father?

Chapter (4)

Young Teenager Queenie Mae Forced to Marry a Stranger

Surely God must have intervened as mom continues, "His wife came home shortly afterward, probably because she wanted to get her water now, and not wait until I returned."

"Great!" I said, feeling some relief for my mother. This pervert will finally be caught, I am thinking to myself. This devil in disguise, Butterfly Jones who is living a terrible lie!

"She passed the bedroom window and she saw her husband attacking me. She rushed into the house and into the bedroom. She accosted her husband, threatening him with death if he ever touched me again," mom said these words with much certainty.

"Mother, that certainly seem as if God arranged for Rose to go to the house at that moment," I replied, anxious to hear what happened next.

"Son, I really believed his wife would have killed him. She was so angry, and her face reflected this intense anger," mother continued as she explained this horrific childhood that she had to endure. No woman wants to be lied to and that is what Butterfly was doing – lying to his wife. Truly, he was a guilty person! Rose E. Jones had believed her husband regarding the first sexual attack incident when Butterfly denied raping Little Queenie.

She told me that her new mom meant those words that she announced with much conviction. She would have killed him because she always carried a small pistol on her person.

The wheels are turning in my head. This is an incredible account of mental or psychological, physical, and sexual abuse on a little girl. How can these adults destroy the young life of a minor? What were their motives when they went to my mother grandmother's home to pick her up? If they did not want to love Little Queenie, they should have left her alone. However, based on my mother words they brought her there to be their little slave. It was never about love. It was never about raising a little girl from childhood to adulthood, to watch her progress like many young people her age. Their objective was evil and devious, especially her new father.

He was devious and he had some despicable plans in mind. He saw a little girl become a blossoming teenager and went after her to an unusual extent. He did not care about her feelings or the results of her psychological or mental well-being after the brutal attacks.

My mother has giving me information so damaging and heartbreaking. She has revealed a despicable character that put on false pretenses to move this youth into his home while she was very young. How could Little Queenie's grandmother possibly know she was putting her granddaughter in harm's way?

I have seen many television shows and read books of these kinds of atrocities on other people. I never would have conceived it happening to one of my loved ones, especially my mother. She did not indicate that Mr. J. C. Jones made any further attempts after getting caught in the act. His dirty deeds unveiled by his second attempt to rape could not possibly occurred again because of her mom threats to kill him. Rose must have been serious, very serious. After listening to mom's final comments, I concluded our conversation for this day. I will call her tomorrow to continue.

I could not wait until the next day. Rather, I called mom after I arrived home. I want to hear about her life after the attacks and the day she met my father. I have eaten dinner and now my mom's phone is ringing.

"Hello mom." I said, as I lay back on my bed, my head resting on my pillow. I proceeded to cross my legs, making myself comfortable. I, Poppa or Rufus need to hear what happens next!

"Hello son. How are you doing?" mom asked.

"I am doing okay, mom" I said in reply.

After our greetings, we continued with my mother's story. My first question was concerning her teen years up to meeting my father. She told me the various abuses kept occurring.

She said, "Mr. J.C. Jones did not assault me anymore after the second attack."

"That is good. I am glad he did not attack you anymore, mother," I told her as I pondered on the intense fear she must have experienced in that terrible house.

"He probably wanted to, but Rose E. Jones would have killed him and buried his big body deep in the woods. Those nine hundred plus acres of land provided countless areas to bury this nasty person," mother continues seemingly excited the rape attempts are finally over. (Actually, mom's parents owned one thousand acres which I later found out). Imagine the wealth my mother could have enjoyed if these were good, honest, and pleasant folks. To the contrary, they were evil hypocrites with sinister motives to do bodily harm to a little girl.

"Poppa, the abuses that continued were mental, threatening, or name-calling, and some physical attacks, slaps to my face and kicking me as if I am a stray dog, "she said reflecting on the terrible and tragic time of her early teenage years. My mother is very expressive with her words. Such an abundance of Common Sense which all of her children inherited! I have recorded all the horrible abuses she has indicated.

What's next?

Before I can ask mom another question, she proceeded to tell me about the arrival of her future husband's father when she turned fifteen-years-old.

"A man you never met before came to your home and claiming to be the father of your future husband?" I asked her. Since, she had described this event some time earlier doing my life. So, I remembered or had foreknowledge about my future dad arrival.

"Yes, one day an old man came to our farm. I have never seen him before. He was in the house talking to Mr. J. C. Jones and Mrs. Rose E. Jones for a short while before they called me to come into the dining room.

"Did he say who he was, mom?" I asked her, anxious to hear more of this individual, my future grandfather.

"The man said his name was Reverend Charlie Louis Brown, and he was a friend of Mr. J. C. Jones. My parents didn't tell me why the old man was there. Maybe they just wanted to introduce me to him. Most likely, they were up to something.

"Now what?" Words probably was flowing through my mother's head when she was asked to come into the dining room area.

Why am I being introduced to this strange old person?

What is Mr. J. C. James and Mrs. Rose Jones up to now?

"My mom and dad did not tell me why he was there, but Reverend Charlie Louis Brown would tell me." Though this man is a Reverend, Teen Queenie Mae still have reservation about him. She does not know this old person sitting in their home.

Mom is precise in the accuracy of her story. This stranger is about to reveal his presence at the home of my mother's parents.

"Poppa, he told me that I was going to be his daughter-in-law. Just like that - out of the blue! I am only fifteen years old, and I am about to become someone's daughter-in-law. A total stranger I have never met before." Surely, Teen Queenie Mae is shocked! Such unimaginable events just continue to occur for this young person, our mother!

"Then, what happened next, mom?" I asked.

"Afterward, this man proceeded to call me to him, and I sat in the chair across from him. He smiled and mentioned it again. My mother and father sat watching but said nothing. They have made up their minds, I would be married off to this man son of whom I knew nothing about." Mother is revealing this, what sounds like a 'shotgun wedding' her parents have decided for her without her consent.

"I have heard of such planned weddings before. It is definitely a 'shotgun wedding' without a shotgun or without a doubt, I concluded in my mind.

"I did not know what to do. I am as scared as I was while living in this mad house with these wicked people, my so-called parents," her voice detailing long term of agonies and despairs. She is behind a rock and a hard place, literally. She is under severe pressures as she approaches her sixteenth birthday. Mom is sitting on pin and needles awaiting this shotgun wedding. She cannot say no to the Joneses' demands. She can only do what she is expecting to do and that is to marry a complete stranger. How would you feel if this happened to you? Just think about it.

Shortly afterward, sometimes later,

"A man walks up the steps to the front door," mom tells me as I listen intently to her mid-teen account of this story. She continues, "This person introduced himself as Mr. Lloyd Brown, the son of Reverend Charlie Louis Brown. He is a farmer from Archer, Florida, a small country town about ten or fifteen miles just outside of Gainesville Florida. He told me that my father has approved of him marrying me. I am young and I do not have any say so in the matter. Mr. J. C. Jones would severely hurt me if I attempted to discourage this wedding event. I could only go along with this shotgun wedding and marry this unknown person of whom I knew nothing about. All I know now is that his father is a Reverend!"

"So son, that is how your mother and father became husband and wife," as she concluded her comment. Then she continued to add more facts about the future start of a new life.

"Mr. Lloyd Brown as I mentioned earlier was a farmer from Archer, Florida and I would become a farmer's wife in the year (1946) mother concludes. The phone went silent but briefly...

Addison, your eldest brother was born on June 15, 1947. Harvey, your second older brother was born on July 24, 1948. But sadly, three months before you, Rufus, Poppa was born on June 23rd, 1949, your father, Lloyd Brown died at the age of forty-four years old from dropsy or edema on March 24, 1949. Lloyd Brown was buried in St. James Missionary Baptist Cemetery in Alachua County. However, all of that is another story.

In addition, let the record show the following historical information. This old man that came to my mother's home named Reverend Charlie Louis Brown of Archer Florida is the father of Mrs. Mahurly Gussie Brown Carrier of the town of Rosewood Florida. The Rosewood Massacre occurred on New Years' Day of 1923. Lloyd Brown, my father is the brother of Mrs. Mahurly Gussie Brown Carrier. We are direct descendants of Reverend Charlie Louis Brown of Archer, Florida. In fact, Addison Brown, our eldest brother resembles his grandfather, Reverend Charlie Louis Brown two hundred percent.

The tragic news of the Rosewood Massacre came as a shock for the family as well as many of the Floridians living in the Northern and Central regions of Florida. The famous American Film Director, Mr. John Singleton felt compel to make a film based on the horrible and tragic events.

I never got to know my father due to his early death. I only know what mom told us, that he was a 'good man.' Finally, something good happens for my mother. She left hatred and entered a world of love. Finally, she has inner peace and do not have to be abused again. Love came knocking at my mother's door and my mother days of abuses ended.

I thanked my mother for providing her son with such an astonishing event but devastating account of her life. She must have been troubled for countless years having it bottled up. The physical abuses has almost destroyed her physical person as evident from the harsh and continual assaults to her person. As I mentioned earlier, her legs and feet reflects the tremendous abuses from hard, physical labor. The broken veins in her legs are evident of the intense laborious life style inflicted upon her by an evil couple.

She has had surgeries on her left eye that was severely damage by her adoptive mother, Mrs. Rose E. Jones when Rose hit Little Queenie Mae with a belt buckle of an old suitcase or trunk. As mom described, "a large buckle from a trunk or suitcase" which she grabbed and hit her in her left eye." Recently, that damaged eye underwent its final surgery and the eye removed. My mother has only one fairly good eye and a lot of courage. I praise her for her ongoing love for all of her children, which now total eight.

This is Mrs. Queenie Mae Brooks-Jones-Brown-Monroe-Myers story of the childhood abuses and the abuses into her teenage years. This is her story for the world to read. Abuses has no time schedule. Abuse is a contagion and as continuous as a raging river. It destroys peace of mind and can have long-lasting feelings of revile. Any time anyone or someone is violated as my mother was violated, the disrespect by maltreatment, the depth of embarrassment and complete terrifying horror of a lifetime will never truly go away. Again, I, Poppa or Rufus Lee Brown ask all and every one of you to dig deep in your hearts and souls. Everyone needs to identify this disgusting behavior and misuse of life called 'Abuse.' It is your God-fearing responsibility to help protect the innocents. Don't allow abusers to continue to roam our planet Earth causing hurt and harm. Stand up and speak out! Do your part for the Prevention of Abuse. Never, but never say it cannot happen to you.

The examples of abuses are numerous, and the numbers continue to grow, even to multiply over time. Help protect the people you love. The cycle for protection goes on and on. You cannot put a deadline on this subject. Do not become a casualty yourself. Take a stand, Now!

The End

In Loving Memory
Of
Mrs. Queenie Mae Myers

Sunrise	*Sunset*
March 5, 1931	*June 23, 2019*

Mother, I dedicate these poems to you, a 'Tribute to a True Queen!' You are our matriarch and true queen, and you are an incredible woman. Thank you for raising your children right. I wrote these poems prior to you presenting me with your story of childhood abuses. It is my way of showing you how much your family appreciates all the love and care you gave to us.

Your Son, Poppa/Rufus Lee Brown...

Poem Number One

It was due to a Lack of Perception why this Book of Poetry is a Dedication to the most important woman I have ever known, my mother, Mrs. Queenie Mae Brooks-Jones-Brown-Monroe Myers.

Yes, it is a long name to go with a long history to which I will explain in my poetic writings. Every poem of poetry refers to a mother willingness to boldly take a stance and survive for her children. Every poem is dedicated to you, mother...

"Mom, How Did You Do It?"

I know your struggles, they were many
yet mom, you wouldn't let that stop you.
Mother, hard times! They were plenty
you sought, fought, even now, still do.
Your head held up high, a simple sigh
Mother Queenie, you just kept on going.
No, never letting anything to deter you
compassionate with love just flowing.
Even to this day, you still remain true
please tell me, how did you do it, mom?
How you complete a tremendous task?
An entire family raised, seven kids on one
you wore a true face and never a mask.
Never heard you complain, how strange
was your love for us kids that stupendous?

During hot summer days and torrent rains
against winds, winter nights, you defend us.
Gee, mom, tell me, how did you do it?
Mom, always you had such a lovely smile.
Guess what mom, I would have blew it
I've probably threw the towel in and howl!

Time traveled; my question never unravel
you had to be the World Greatest Mom!
Just how you did it like collegiate Scrabble
wow mother, gee, you have a puzzled son.
Always, it was work, work, and more work
I never ever saw you having just fun mom
The well-being of your children was first
its mornings and evenings were never done.
Around the clock, I'm just mildly speaking,
you kept on keeping on like a rising sun.
Gee whiz, how did you do it, mother?
Mother, will I ever unravel this mystery?
I would no doubt have thrown the shoe in
the life you lived seems like a risk to me.
Yes, you prevailed, gee, you did swell!
all of your kids have grew to adulthood.
Thinking of your life, I would have bail
I know mom, I know, that ain't good.
Courageously and bold you stood firm
you born us and raised us to adulthood.

Mom Queenie, I can remember it all
in my memory, as if it was yesterday.
Poppa, remember you going to work
for you, it was all work and no play.
Yes, I remember, all the consistency
weary, dreary to provide for your kids
all your diligence and your empathy
it didn't matter what the white man did,
or display nor say or tried to do away
mom, I remember unmatched courage
that same courage you possess today.
Still, I just wish I knew how you did it?
No, never, ever did you leave us alone
Through common sense, many outwitted
"Let he who hasn't sin cast the 1st stone!"
No, never, ever did you back down
from doing what you knew to be right.
Mom, today if Life was a Smackdown
you would still put up a good fight,
while keeping the truth into the light!"

Mother, you became a miracle worker
moreover, your miracles became real.
Through hard time and never a deserter
til this day, you haven't desert us still.
Mom, food was always on our table
as pots and pans rattled in the kitchen
Proverbs speak of the woman capable
and mother you have my full attention.
Neither hard times, drought, or dread

could never hold its own against you
many miracles continued to perform
no matter how or what you been thru.
Mother, even the amazing MacGyver
would praise you for things you done
he would shower you with accolades
contending that you are Number One.
So, yes, yes mother, I keep on typing
pressing on keypads on the keyboard.
I type with heartfelt love, I type this
about my mother, A Queen I so adore.

Yes mom, you led a remarkable life
adoption then losing your blood family
Starting a new life with total strangers
and I speak the truth though, candidly.
It is what it is, that is how it happened
at seven-years old, in a strange world.
Start of your new life all over, minus
brothers and sister to share your world.
You should have led a wonderful life
your new mother was a schoolteacher.
You should've lived in a happy world
but your new dad a monstrous creature.
In spite of it, you made it thru all that
you married, and then we came along.
Sadly, our dad died, and that was that
three little boys to raise on your own.
Then later on mom, you had more kids,
Mom another boy and girls to care for

but you never gave up on motherhood
rather, you proved who you really are.

When I got older and began to reason
then, I could see with mine own eyes
many struggles throughout the season
still, keeping your eyes on the prize.
That prize prove to be your children
it mattered not what; or why or how
you stood firm like a fortified pillar
the same fortitude that you have now.
Yes, mom tell me, how did you do it?
Even in our teenage years undaunted
no barrier, bridge you couldn't cross
you got your kids what they wanted.
Despite the fact, dad Lloyd, you lost
as time moved forward unrelentless
put even more history now behind us
thru the good and bad times in stress.
It was in your God you truly put trust
too many times mom, tired and weak.
Mother, you refuse to let that stop you
as tired, weary, and weak met defeat
mother nothing negative got through.

Your children, now men and women
now living all over these United States
and yes, our love for you is continuous
you keep living no matter what it takes.
Mom, you provided an exemplary model

it was how to be a winner and never quit.
You exemplified and we are not startled
because you exercised smarts and wits.
From a youth to teen, then to adulthood
this question still continue to baffle me
Mom, how in the world did you do it?
and wow, mother handled it all masterly.
Surely mom, goodness will follow you
because you always walked in the light.
Gee whiz, I wish I had that follow thru
maybe, one day, even someday I might.
What you have done is most wonderful
so, I honor you and I keep you in sight
it would be sin for me not to honor you,
after all of the things and all of the hype.
So, yes, mother, I continue to honor you
and yes mom, your son continue to write.

I can see you even when you are not here
I can see and feel your love, crystal clear.
There is none like you, anywhere, no how
I can gladly say this and so I say it now.
From on the rooftop, I Pop can proclaim,
hey, this's my mom, Queenie is her name!
In the path of righteousness Queenie walk
the Word of God on her lips when she talk.
To teach what's good, preach what's right
wickedness mom abhor, I can gladly cite.
You turn from darkness and love the light
you set good examples, as evil take flight.

Your discussions what you truly believe in
always about good, to turn away from sin.
I hear you even when you are not around
I hear God's words of uprightness abounds.
The glory of the Lord even a whisper a hiss
your love for God amazing yes believe this.
I am glad to cite, glad to write, glad to type
my mom loves truths like dark love nights.

(Copyright 2022 Rufus Lee Brown)
Written 2007 by Rufus Lee Brown

Poem Number Two

Mrs. Queenie Mae led a life of pains and misery. At the age of seven-years old, given up for adoption to a married Black couple, a schoolteacher, and a postal worker. These people, this couple of influential status promise Little Queenie Mae's grandmother that she will receive an education and will go to a college or university. All that was a lie! A big fat lie...

"Through the Eyes of a Son"

Please, picture with your mind's eye
a struggling mother trying to get by.
But first, picture with me, if you will
no frills, thrills what's written is real.
Picture a young girl with no options
is given up by parents for adoption.
Separate, alone in a brand-new home
a new family which to call her own.
A new dad a Postman, Butterfly Jones
mom a schoolteacher, Rosa E. Jones
Queenie Mae, her maiden name Brooks
a brand-new life and different outlook.
Picture a young girl starting over again
an only child out to make new friends.
Yet, there will be no fun for my mom
see with me through the Eyes of a Son.

Come with me on a voyage to the past
see, see what I see, try not to be last.
A journey will bring us to realization
Queenie Mae and life's complications.
Look, can you see all her parents' land
an seven-years old trying to understand.
Parents accumulate lots of possessions
thousand acres of land, no protections.
Can you see, Queenie got a baby colt?
"I name you Bandit!" she happily spoke.
Together they grew, a colt, a little girl
this is Queenie's horse, A Queen's World.
Do you see what I see, the two together?
Can you see 'er Bandit riding for shelter?
She has skills y 'all look at Queenie ride
do you picture this thru her Son's Eyes?

Little Queen is thirteen-years of age now
see with me as Queenie try not to frown.
See that huge fella that's treating her bad
he's Butterfly Jones, it's her adopted dad.
He is so big, and must weigh 300 pounds
"Don't hit my mom!" Queenie fall down.
Her mom Rosa, a teacher must be timid
stand helpless by, seem her powers limit.
Little Queenie Mae stout, bold and brave
Queenie is adopted to be the Jones slave.
Mistreatments can't be claimed to be just
yet, she struggles to live, Queenie a must.
Queenie, a survivor with a lot of courage

see with me she refuse to be discouraged.
See that tough girl, hey, that is my Mom
see with me through the Eyes of a Son!

Queenie has turned fifteen years of age
she is getting older a start of a new page.
Life brings changes as we shall all see
a guest came to the home, who can it be?
See what I see, believe what you behold
he is there for mother is what I am told.
Her daddy is giving up this teenage girl
hand in marriage; What in the world??
Hey, it is Lloyd Brown, he's Poppa dad
yes, way back in them days it's the fad.
Mother did not have a choice, no voice
it's a shotgun wedding her dad endorse.
Wow, my mother, she looks so frighten
would you expect her to be enlighten?
I'm midway in this poem and not done
travel with me thru the Eyes of a Son.

The first embryo is seeded at sixteen
it's Addison to fulfill daddy's dream.
A year later out came son number two
Harvie's born and now mom has a few.
Dad is a farmer, his health is not good
forty-four yo it's not quite understood.
Oops! It's Pop time, I am in the uterus
caught by a midwife it was done to us.
Not one hospital, none in the vicinity

lands in the country fill with serenity.
Soon another son has joined the scene
his name is Johnnie, a four-baby team.
Daddy died, no time to communicate
I am a newborn that was Poppa's fate.
See what I see, it is more then, some
picture it through the - Eyes of a Son.

Threatening by death, we pack and left
moved to Gainesville or be put to death.
Mom has comradeship, now its two girls
entered Gloria and Mary into the world.
Complicated, Mary is soon adopted too
gone like a space shuttle aboard its crew.
Do you see tears glisten in mom eyes?
They are for real yet still my mom rise!
Enters George Monroe, the family told
here to rescue mom so claimed his goal.
Slides in mom's heart and the two wed
George a hard worker so the family fed.
Eventually, George packs everyone up
and we move to Orlando minus a truck.
See what Pop see, it is more than, one
See the picture thru the Eyes of a Son.

Life keep moving forward a son is born
So cute our little brother, and lot of fun.
Bobby's his name wow he's born white
did a wrong kid come home this night?
Soon, George started cheating on mom

always running the streets & havin fun.
Soon after we were able to buy a house
money mom save and not mom spouse.
Yeah, I got a baby sis, shut my mouth
She's lite as Bobby, Rose in the house!
See all the crazy ruckus, it was not fun
looky, look through the Eyes of a Son.

(Copyright 2022 Rufus Lee Brown)
Written 2005 by Rufus Lee Brown

Poem Number Three

A Dedication to Mrs. Queenie Mae, Our Mother
"Thank you, Father for giving us a Mother so strong
thank you for giving her all the strengths to prolong.
Thank you, Jehovah because of your love she strive
provided for her kids because of her we all survived.

"Mother, This is Your Hour!"

Mother, so magnificent in your abilities
and you fulfilled all your children needs.
Despite all the many hardships, mother
dear, you, you were more than equipped.
You raised your children on your own
for all of us, mom til your children grown.
The portrait you painted, it still remains
such a perfect example you never change.
Mom, in your God Jehovah you put trust
never rely on man and never spirit crush.
Head's up, never gave up, stand straight
we never hunger for, food on our plates.
You were a stronghold when life quake
you are like gold, the finest and not fake.
When God made you, wonderfully made
spread your arms, providing much shade.
Who's that standing in the Watchtower?
That's you, Mother - this be your Hour!

There would be days, all seem hopeless
there were times, when cold – coatless.
Through many struggles and the hassles
anywhere with you became our castle.
No high school education, you succeed
yet, no riches, love is what we needed.
By your lonesome kept food on the table
and I write about you, truths no fables.
Qualities of you is describe in Proverbs
a mother fulfill King Solomon's words.
Never were you contentious nor conceit
mother you kept us, gladly a son repeat.
Thoughtful, a stronghold, so we roll on
all years ahead, let her story be told on.
Mom, you stood firm and through it all
God blessed you and you heed his call.
Seasons came, spring, summer, and fall
in winter, magnificent, mom stands tall.
Who's that standing in the Watchtower?
That's you, Mother - this be your Hour!

Love you gave your kids, stupendous
when sick, you mend as you attend us.
Though stressed out, you stayed true
there are a lot of moms yet, only you
and when there came time of changes
I grin, you made ashamed, shameless.
Though, she lived in a college town
it is common sense that you abound,
doing what you had to for your kids

and we do appreciate all that you did.
Even until this day when stressed out
your counsel and vision's the best out.
Through the bad times and good time
a strong mother, I write these rhymes.
So, we appreciate all that you've done
with you in our corner we always won.
Who's that standing in the Watchtower?
That's you, Mother this be your Hour!

(Copyright 2022 Rufus Lee Brown)
Written 2005 by Rufus Lee Brown

Poem Number Four

A Dedication to Mrs. Queenie Mae, Our Mother
"Thank you for the peace, the harmony, and your blessings
for the power of your love, O' God, nullified the stressing.
There's much more to be said to offer praise to you, Mom
accept this dedication from all your daughters and sons...

"Mother, Our Mother!"

You've been very good to us
and you really taught us well.
You never treated us unjust
so sweet to us so easy to tell.
Our lives, we owe all to you
mom, you were always kind.
To us all, you remained true
you've given us all your time.

Mother, Our Mother
we love you so much,
yes, Mom and Mother
you're a proven crutch.
Mother, Our Mother
you took a firm stand.
Mom, compared to you
there's none in the land.

Many times, you shed tears
mom, so many times indeed.
Yet still you stuck with us
so, in life we would succeed.
Always, God will bless you
for your many good deeds.
Many of times in want, still
you sought to fulfill our need.
Mom, you were always there
love for your kids, immense.
Ours were your concern mom
past, present, and future tense.

Mother, Our Mother
we love you so much,
yes, Mom and Mother
you're a proven crutch.
Mother, Our Mother
you took a firm stand.
Mom, compared to you
there's none in the land.

If Pop become wealthy and
I gained many riches, mom,
your life I would surely make
sunny, believe it, it'll be fun.
Mom, I would take good care
because you are A Queen.
Mom, so much Pop will do

to fulfill all of your dreams.
All the lows or out-of-place
Poppa will certainly erase.

(Copyright 2022 Rufus Lee Brown)
Written 2017 Rufus Lee Brown

POEM NUMBER FIVE

Let's start at the very beginning and why not? Let's go back to the birth date of this wonderful person and A True Queen, my Mother. She is born on March 5, 1931, to parents, Mr., and Mrs. Fannie Mae Brooks. She had brothers and one other sister name Pauline, a twin to her older brother who birth first, Paul.

"Mirror, Mirror On the Wall!"

Mom forfeited an education of school
denied by ignorant and ruthless fools.
No, never, ever, ever did Queenie quit
Lloyd Brown died; she raised her jits.
She work real hard, making ends meet
that meant walks to work on tired feet.
Those secular jobs paid for food to eat
mother kept moving when ill or weak.
Babysitting kiddies good, bad ones too
cleaning for the rich, mother had to do.
Mrs. Queenie Mae did whatever it took.
sometime stuck working for bad crooks.
Whenever you look into a mirror, Mom
'stare at yourself with pride, says a son.
Mom, you are the greatest of them all!
The greatest and true, gladly stand tall.

Mirror, Mirror On the Wall
Who's greatest mother of them all!
It's Mrs. Queenie haven't you heard,
that's the latest news, Word!

At an early age, yo mistakes were made
but that is what imperfection is all about.
Never did Queenie let her dreams fade
and my mother, weathered the drought.
Her heartless stepfather, Butterfly Jones
gave Teen Queenie hand up in marriage.
That is how Queenie married Pop's dad,
at fifteen years of age, life was ravaged.
One after another, three boys were born
three little ones to carry on Lloyd legacy.
Alone and on her own, a life that's scorn
takin care of children, she now has three.
Whenever you look in a mirror, Mother
'stare at yourself with pride, says a son
Mom, you are the greatest of them all!
The greatest and true, gladly stand tall.

Mirror, Mirror On the Wall
Who's greatest mother of them all!
It's Mrs. Queenie haven't you heard,
that's the latest news, Word!

Mother, all the abuse that you endured
would have broken the backs of many.
Years of abuse from your adopted folks
mom a beatdown would surprise a-plenty.
Attempted rape by a man you call father
the first and second attempt to you fail.
God could have led evil to be slaughter
and allow this evil pedophile rot in hell.
He escaped the rape far as I am concern
but someone even greater was watching.
Not only rot in hell but like a fire burn
Serious mom, this son Pop not joshing.
Whenever you look in a mirror, Mother
'stare at yourself with pride, says a son.
Mom, you are the greatest of them all!
the greatest and true, proudly stand tall.

Written 2005 by Rufus Lee Brown

POEM NUMBER SIX

Times must have been difficult during those days from the birth period of this adorable little girl because when she turned seven-years old, she is given up for adoption. That would be the worst thing that her grandmother could have done, so unknowingly...

"Mother Queenie is Oooo-La-La!"

Hey there mother, it's Pop and I am back
writing rhymes in a world that is whack.
The world is crazy like ten cats in a sack
my poems the beginning of the first act.
When I'm done composing these rhymes,
a Book of you will conclude these lines.
Ooo-La-La mom, how am I doing so far?
These words of love is Hooray Hoo-Raa.
Mother is what some of yo kids call you
yet I call you mom that is how Poppa do.
I guess I 've been different to an extent
I guess that's how our lives were meant.
I included Ebonics call Black folks slangs
this is how Poppa write, Pop do his thing.
You are our Queen and our favorite star
yo reign in our lives made it Ooo-La-La!

You shouldered responsibilities for years,
outdid, outdone all of your closes peers.

Never dropped the ball dogged out all fears.
When enemies call you appalled their jeers.
On the summit, we appoint you the Queen B
all your children, not only RLB, that be me.
Though, I do all the writings, I write for all
your kids have talents, writing was my call.
You are a pillar and a force to be dealt with
factually, Pop know that it is Jehovah's gift.
As the Perfect Foreteller he laid out a plan
the Omni-Potent, thru it all you still stand.
He saw in you what none, no one could see
a magnificent creature mom, you, Queen B.
Ha! I've see none, no notta, mother by far
I applaud you, so that makes it Ooo-La-La!

'Mother' a name some of your kids call you
so, I write to retain, to frame, I applaud you.
'Mom' a name the older & youngest as well.
while other kids are from a different shell.
We share a common passion, and it is true
we got agape' for us and got agape' for you.
Mother, I have retained all of the glad parts
and Poppa have eliminated all the sad parts,
my purpose a reminder a mom's glad heart
Let's face it --- Mother or Mom or Momma
and all that makes up all the - Ooo-La-Las!!

Written 2005 by Rufus Lee Brown

Poem Number Seven

Fate was not a given of goodness or kindness, but shame.
Destiny proved not glorious but shamefully painful.
Little Queenie Mae would not share growth with brothers
and only sister, Pauline. She would be detached from her
siblings and blood parents. Here is more poetry as it opens
more doors...

"The Whole Truth and Nothing but the Truth!"

You been there for us, your daughters, and sons
you shed your love upon us, life with you was fun.
This is the Whole Truth and Nothing but the Truth
from the time of our birth and all thru our youth,
your children loves you and your love was a boost
we all needed to carry us through the many years
you never let us down through hardship and tears.
We are grateful without you we would have failed
you maintained discipline and it kept us out of jail.
A single Mom the yoke you bore didn't break you
it made you strong that's why these words are true.
Your struggles paid off none of your kids are weak
all are strong adults and our love for you runs deep.
This the Whole Truth and a dedication to you, Mom
A Poem of Appreciation from Daughters and Sons.

This is the Whole Truth and Nothing but the Truth,
born to you from embryos to give you your 'Juice.
When I say 'Juice' it means wholehearted respect,
you earned it because you kept your kids in check.
Kept a watchful eye so no one would do us harm
as a hen does her chicks, safety under your arms.
When we did bad things, it caught your attention
never did you swear that's a fact I had to mention.
Though, our father died, you took on the to lead
that was a colossal task and mother you succeed.
All your kids are alive, and we owe that all to you
you did so much more, these words are too few.
You relied on no man you followed a higher plan
Jehovah carried us, blessed us with open hands.
This the Whole Truth and Nothing but the Truth
A Tribute to a True Queen and wisdom a boost...

I conclude these writings, let the Truth be known
thank you because you never, ever led us wrong.
You would give us the last clothing off your back
we never went hungry; these words are true facts.
Materialism not your forte' kept our lives on track
provided the essentials in a world terribly whack.
You never pull false strings never nothing strange
you set a good example, your kids never ashame.
You maintain your spirituality in a God, you trust
frown at bad, out of truth, not because you must.
So, much to live for grands & great grands, too
none would be possible at all if it wasn't for you.
Your seed has multiplied, and legacy will live on

"A Capable Woman" King Solomon had prolong.
Jehovah, a loving God and let your days be long
followed did will, obeyed words written in stone.
The family tree have grown and has taken roots
this the Whole Truth and Nothing but the Truth...

Written 2005 by Rufus Lee Brown

Poem Number Eight

In honor of my mother Mrs. Queenie Mae Brooks-Jones-Brown-Monroe Myers this poem book is being dedicated. A strong Black female that travel through hell and came out victorious. Her Lord and God would ensure Queenie no longer suffer from man's hand. He carried her through the rest of her journeys under the safety of his wings...

"They Should Have Followed Your Path"

Mom, where are they now as I look around?
Where the same people that put you down?
Remember 'em as we moved town to town?
Places we grew up, where we're living now.
It all begin when you were young at heart
married early that is when your life started.
Back in the day before life really changed
and Satan went crazy started doing things.
Young girls had babies in their early teens
the differences they were married, it seem.
The past, I won't blasting it's how it went
married our dad, not a given, nor accident
You had your first child tender age sixteen
and became a mother, became Mrs. Queen.
A married mother, despite what life mean,
along came others almost a baseball team
Daddy passed away - a dent in your dream
came the ridicules country folks it seemed

Yet those that jeered how long did they last?
Mom they should have Followed your Path.

You never quit, we move to grandma house
life was not easy at all - living in the South.
Your hands full with things the kids needed
unlike others in life mother, you succeeded.
The silly gossip and stupid talk came along
of your life and all things, you done wrong.
Neighbors, relatives and those close to you
had something to say to make your life blue.
Enter a Black Knight and gather your crew
moved to Orlando, where many of us grew.
Good things came at first, a hubby, so true
like most men, hubby did as most men do.
He began okay, taking us out the Projects
for that Pop gives him my deepest respect.
The project ladies spoke negatively - they
Ms. Suzie a lady that lived across the way?
Then there's Ms. B, a next-door neighbor
I think project ladies all of 'em lack flavor.
Yet, all the women that talked all that trash
Mom they should have Followed your Path.

Jehovah said "Queenie, you will not fail!"
you and your kids, all of you will prevail."
Well, he didn't falter never left you alone
Jehovah is never slow and never do wrong.
Despite good deeds, a good life you lived
they jealous of you cause you live to give.

Saying nothing nice as you moved away
Queen this and that, negative all they say.
Where's the busybodies? They didn't last,
Mom they should 've Followed your Path.

(Copyright 2021 Rufus Lee Brown)
Written 2005 by Rufus Lee Brown

Poem Number Nine

Tribute to my Mother, A True Queen
"You Bet Not Cry!" and "I Will Never Forget – Amidst the Thorns and Thistles" both novels written for mom and about my mom are available at book stores of Barnes & Nobles, Amazon, Google, and Walmart as well as other book store establishments. These two novels were published by Xlibris Publishing Company and have been available since 2016.

"Mother Queenie Keeps Going, Going, Going"

I see you Mom and I wonder if
I too one day will display your gift.
Mother, I wonder as I watch you go
on, on and on yo, who's the true pro.
Years I notice abilities you possessed,
established yourself with much success.
Though up in years that didn't stop you
Energizer Bunny, your time is through.
Mom got you beat like the skies be blue
you had a long run now you're through.
Your reign has ended so just step aside
your reign descended so just step aside.
Mom has ascended and she's got stride
walk away Pink Bunny keep your pride.
I got to give credit where credit is due
you been upended now you're through.
Your drum banging boing, boing, boing,

can't match my mom,
she keep going, going, going.

Gee whiz, I commend you Pink Bunny
you help a lot of rich folks bank money
You are in commercials and many ads
drum banging made stockholders glad.
All over the planet, you have been seen
your drum bang is a successful scheme.
Sporting shades, displaying your brand
Geico Gecko next to you cannot stand.
A New Superior Woman on the scene
she's our Mother her name Mrs. Queen.
Queenie Mae Myers, she is energized
three days of the week it is no surprise,
she walks treadmill doing her exercise
strengthen her heart a course that's wise.
Hail the Queen! Pink Bunny,
and your drum boing,
the Queen is on the scene
just going, going, going.

So starts an episode of a fresh new face
Mrs. Queenie Mae done took your place.
She has taken your place, so you are out
beating on your drums round and about.
You see, she's not going to let her ill rule
she recognizes in your shades, you cool.
You keep going putting others to shame
you ruled the world until my mom came.

So, bodacious and the world loves you
Mom is gracious the world loves her too.
Bang on Pink Bunny pound those drums
your reign is over, replaced by our Mom.
You're welcome to share her glory, join
our Mom just keep going,
going, going, and going......

(Copyright 2022 Rufus Lee Brown)
Written 2005 by Rufus Lee Brown

POEM NUMBER TEN

Poem after poem I wrote in honor of a magnificent woman, my mother Mrs. Queenie Mae Brooks-Jones-Brown-Monroe Myers. Books of suffering by a seven-year-old into her teen years and early adulthood by savages that portray themselves as good folks. Tribute A Queen, a Survivor, my Mom...

"Mother Queenie, A True Queen and Matriarch!"

At eighty-six, she sits at her front doorway
views the world go by each and every day.
Unable to walk outside so she sits and stare
anytime visited she sits in her favorite chair.
Once, was A Queen that could hold her on
lived for her kids until they were all grown.
Lover of righteousness she was never alone
she trust in her God, making God her own.
Queenie a proud mother her kids, she boast
proudly, she says 'Jehovah she loves most.'
She don't walk in the dark, but in the light
not against man, but against evil she fights.
She has proven herself time and time again
prayers are heard, God's angels her friend.
She's a strong Black woman until the end
she loves doing right, a hundred times ten.

Eighty-six, she sit staring out 'er front door
her health failed her many problems, galore.
Mrs. Queenie, a Survivor, fights for her life
despite illnesses, and the rolling of the dice.
She is a Matriarch, every sense of the word
lives for her kids like the bees and the birds.
Her health problems, far too many to name
I will name a few that will drive most insane.
Diabetes is her deadliest disease of them all
a piece of a heart (3) heart surgeries I recall.
Her right knee osteoarthritis tween the bones
she roll in her chair cannot walk on her own.
Total blind in her left eye so it was removed
Mom's hearing departing she sings no blues.
Suffers with blood pressures that climbs high
so, aware with age that her frailty, multiply.

Queen, True Matriarch despite the illnesses
refuses to give up, every day, a fight to live.
Queenie a fighter, she's still remains strong
sons and daughters left, living on their own.

She had dogs, Martii and a dog name Rock
she loved them two dogs so much non-stop.
My granddaughter love dogs just as she did
Amelia 'Millie' got (2) dogs and just as big.
Great-great grandma Queenie, she love you
I am happy y 'all met, wow how time flew.

Queen, True Matriarch despite the illnesses
refuses to give up, every day, a fight to live.
Queenie a fighter, she's still remains strong
sons and daughters left, living on their own.

Bobby was your baby boy, but died in 2014
we miss him the other half of my road team.
A 'very good son' who's life end, too soon
we loved him very much, them days gloom.

(Copyright 2022 Rufus Lee Brown)
Written 2018 by Rufus Lee Brown

POEM NUMBER ELEVEN

Mom, I wrote a poetic song "I Will Always Remember" by Rufus Lee Brown to you. Mother, I could go on and on writing of all the good things I love about you. I would be sitting here typing for a very long time. But before I conclude, please allow me to continue clarifying other wonderful things, which have made me, us, so proud of you.

"I Will Always Remember!"

I will always remember
all the love and good deeds
you did for your children in
the past and present, too.
I will always remember
the courage and fortitude
of you and how you have
endured over the years.
I will always remember
the compassion shown to
all of us, despite the many
trials and tribulations, you
faced daily, so bravely.
I will always remember
your many struggles, yet
you sought and fought
to get through them all.

I will always remember
when 'hard times' heaped
itself upon you, you took it
upon yourself, and you
accepted those challenges
and became our champion.
I will always remember
a beautiful smile on your
face when life felt good to
you. It was a precious and
happy smile, I will always
remember.
I will always remember
you always wore a true
face daily. You never
masked your appearance
to please your opposition.
I will always remember
a mother never complaining
no matter how strange the
situation might be.

I will always remember
a mother that would not
allow situations to deter
her from making all the
correct choices, especially
if it involved her children.
I will always remember
a mother whose love was

so stupendous, no matter
how severe times or the
events that befall us.
I will always remember
and I still need to know
'How Did You Do It?' Your
struggles were many, yet,
you remained intact.
I will always remember
a mother like 'Atlas holding
the World' on his shoulders.
A strong woman, always.

I will always remember
the days and nights you
would sacrifice for your
children, when illness was
abound. You placed your
children first to ensure
they remained sound.
I will always remember
your mornings and your
evenings were never done.
You took care of matters
at home and abroad too.
I will always remember
how round the clock, you?
just keep on going like the
famous "Energizer Bunny.
I will always remember

that whenever you did
have fun, it was with your
children and I apologize for
being the child that gave you
the most headaches.

I will always remember
a mother that worked many
jobs when necessary to work
to provide for her children's
every want and need.
I will always remember
a mother severely abused
yet, she became a good
mother despite her pains
and suffering growing up.
I will always remember
a mother always working.
Mom, did you have any
fun at all, I try to recall.
Was it laughter for you,
the times spent with us?
I will always remember
how your neighbors would
mock you, mentally, just
because you were different.
They could not understand
that you were not a street
woman, but a loving and
caring woman and mother.

I will always remember
a mother very truthful. A
mother who put her God
first in her life and whom
always worshipped him.
I will always remember
you mother, making the
good decisions. A mother
which wanted her kids
to grow up appreciating
God as our Heavenly
Father for all mankind.
I will always remember
that when your adoptive
mother, Rosa Jones came
to live with us, you never
disrespect or mistreated
her despite all the abuses
she inflicted upon you.
I will always remember
my mother having Bible
studies with the kids we
grew up with in Carver
Court Projects. They were
good times for us and for
them as well. Your heart
was always open to help
others.

I will always remember
your stand for righteousness
and truth while others
around you indulged in doing
bad things, you would always
remain faithful to your God.
I will always remember
when your second eldest
son was shot nine times in
his own bedroom, in his home
in the city of Orlando Florida
how you dropped whatever that
you were doing at the time to
to sit with and care for him
in the hospital, making sure
that he came through the
many surgeries to save his
life. You were dedicated to
all your children.

I will always remember
when our Bobby became ill,
you dropped everything
and drove to Orlando and
you took him with you back
to Gainesville. You admitted
him in the Alachua General
Hospital. If one more day
had passed, our brother
would have died here in

Orlando. Mother, you saved
Bobby's life and we Love
you extremely for doing that.
Bobby had no awareness
his life was in jeopardy.
You saved him, mother!
I will always remember
and I Will Never Forget!
a Mother's Love for her
family. To this day at the
age of (87) you continue
to live for your children.
I will always remember
your dream to become a
doctor, yet that dream was
shattered by the ones that
imposed upon you a life of
a slave rather than allow you
go to school like your peers."

I will always remember
how so eloquently and with
clarity, you spoke. Mom, you
could communicate with Rulers
of Nations. You could easily
sit and chit-chat with Barbara
Walters or Oprah Winfrey
and they would praise you.
I will always remember
your love for your pet dogs,

Rock and Martii. Your dogs
earned your respect and you
truly cared for them. Should
someone step on a single
blade of grass in your yard,
they would alert you with a
growl or bark without fail.
I will always remember
that life for you was not
Chance but life always had
its purpose. You placed your
children on a pedestal and
God rewarded you for it."

(Copyright 2021 Rufus Lee Brown)
Written 2018 by Rufus Lee Brown

Poem Number Twelve

Mother Queenie Mae Brooks-Jones-Brown-Monroe Myers was a Strong Black Woman that lived a terrible life as a child, teenager and into early adulthood. She was forced to marry a stranger – my father Lloyd Brown at the age of sixteen. She had no idea if this man was good or evil. Remember, her newly acquired parents were the worst folks in all of Alachua County. My mom suffered at their hands and vowed 'never to forget and neither will I, her son, Rufus Lee Brown, and the writer of her destructive life. In my mother's own words, I write sad memories and a few glad times...

"I Will Never Forget!"

I will never forget my mother
Fannie Mae Brooks and the love
she shown to me before she
went to be with her Lord.
I will never forget the precious
moments that I spent with my
brothers and sisters when I lived
with them in Jacksonville before
I was taken away to be raised
by grandmother, Julia Whitfield.
I will never forget my grandmother's love for me prior to
her giving me up for adoption
which, she hoped for and she

thoroughly believed I would
get a proper education with
my new adoptive parents."

I will never forget missing
out on the opportunity to go
to school in Duval County,
Jacksonville Florida along
with my brothers and sisters.
I will never forget the day
that Julia Whitfield gave me
to strangers, two strange folks
which I never met before.
I will never forget seeing my
adoptive father for the very
first time. The stranger I saw
was tall, jet-black skin color,
red eyes, a giant-of-a-man.
He frightened me so much,
I ran to hide in the outhouse
behind the main house.

I will never forget watching
grandmother Julia Whitfield
for the last time as my adoptive
parents drove away.
I will never forget when my
adoptive parents brought me to
my new home for the very first
time and they made me sleep on

a little cot in the dining room as
several bedrooms remained
empty for more than a year.
I will never forget my adoptive
parents deny me the opportunity
to go to school until I was nine
years old. I was brought to their
home and put to work on their
large farm full of animals.

I will never forget my adoptive
parents working me as if I was
their slave girl than a daughter.
I will never forget all the beatings
that Butterfly Jones and his wife
would inflict upon me then dare
me, saying, "you bet not cry!"
I 'll never forget Butterfly Jones
tying me to a tree then, would
whip me with his cow's whip.
I will never forget my mother
Rose E. Jones striking me in
my left eye with a buckle of
an old trunk's belt she had.
I will never forget Butterfly
Jones tying me on occasions
and stand there watching as
his wife beat me with peach
tree limbs tied together with
tobacco strings.

I will never forget their words
repeatedly ringing loud and
clear to me, you bet not cry!
over and over again after
causing bodily harm to my
head, my face and my body.
I will never forget my precious
horse, Bandit, and the many fun
times that we shared together.
I will never forget riding high
in the saddle on Bandit as he
would leap and jump fences
on Butterfly Jones property.
I will never forget the day a
water moccasin came across
Bandit's path and my horse
stomp the snake with its hoofs.

I will never forget the trickery
and cunning of my adoptive
father taking me in the woods
on his vast property to molest
and rape me. This pedophile I
called daddy, Butterfly Jones.
I will never forget his wife, Rose
E. Jones slapping me to my face
with her hand hard after I told
her Butterfly Jones tried to rape
me in the deep woods on the
family's massive property.

I will never forget the blood left
on my saddle from him violating
me in the woods to my private
area putting his huge finger
up inside of my vagina.

I will never forget the day
that Butterfly Jones put my
life in jeopardy by telling me
to hide, then to shoot Mister
Whitehurst with a .22 rifle
while we were at the bridge
that separate their property.
I will never forget soon after
that incident at the bridge,
even though I was in hiding
to protect him from Mister
Whitehurst, he tied me to a bed
so, his wife, Rose could beat
me with peach-tree limbs tied
together with tobacco-strings.

I will never forget Butterfly
Jones calling me the many
terrible and horrible names
as I grew up in their home.
I will never forget the hurt
and harm caused to me by
Bo Diddley and his two co-
workers. They kill a chicken

that belonged to Butterfly
Jones and lied that I did it.
I will never forget being tied
to a tree and being beaten
with his cow's whip as Bo
Diddley and his co-workers
watched and grinned.
I will never forget how cruel
people can be just because
you do not lower your morals
to satisfy their evil needs.

I will never forget being
forced into a marriage to a
stranger, to a strange man
without having my consent.
I will never forget after your
father Lloyd died, Butterfly
Jones struck me hard in the
head with the handle of a
hammer, which left a dent
or mark on my head.
I will never forget in the
Fall of 1949 when Butterfly
Jones fell ill and had to be
admitted in the hospital
in Gainesville. I will never
forget the look on Butterfly
Jones' face while he laid
in that bed and he saw Mr.

Whitehurst standing in his
hospital doorway. Mister
Whitehurst stood there and
stared at Butterfly Jones.

I will never forget the shark-
like eyes of Mr. Whitehurst,
like that of a tiger shark or
lion ready to attack its prey.
I will never forget watching
Mr. Whitehurst and Butterfly
Jones' physician having a
conversation the same early
morning at the nurse station.
I will never forget watching
Butterfly doctor hand his nurse
a silver tray with a small brown
pill on it. Then she brought that
small brown pill to Butterfly's
hospital room and handed it to
him to consume with water.
She would remain in his room
to watch him take the death pill.
I will never forget Butterfly
Jones died moments later the
same day within a few hours
after swallowing that small
brown pill administered to
him by the hospital's nurse.

I will never forget seeing him
lying in his bed, dead, with his
red-eyes open wide, the same
devil-like red eyes that frighten
me for so many years.

I will never forget the
feeling of utter relief. It
was overwhelming feeling
of freedom, being relieved
knowing I will never suffer
because of this man existence.
I will never forget watching
his wife, Rose Jones shedding
many tears after her husband,
Butterfly Jones had died.
I will never forget I did not
shed a single teardrop as he
laid up in that hospital bed,
dead with his red eyes open.

Mother tells me that she hoped someone would write about this, her life, and its many struggles. "Son, it was very important for me to remember my life in the home of my adoptive parents. No one should ever experience all the mayhems, I had to endure."

www.ingramcontent.com/pod-product-compliance
Lightning Source LLC
Chambersburg PA
CBHW071103120626
46546CB00003B/1258